What's in the WEST?

By Robert Walker

Crabtree Publishing Company

www.crabtreebooks.com

Crabtree Publishing Company

www.crabtreebooks.com

Author: Robert Walker
Publishing plan research and development:
    Sean Charlebois, Reagan Miller
    Crabtree Publishing Company
Editor: Lynn Peppas
Proofreader: Crystal Sikkens
Editorial director: Kathy Middleton
Photo research: Crystal Sikkens
Designer: Ken Wright
Production coordinator: Ken Wright
Prepress technician: Ken Wright
Print coordinator: Katherine Berti

Photographs:
Bigstock: page 23 (top)
Dreamstime: pages 9, 18
Keystone Press: © Gary Braasch/Zuma:
    page 21 (right)
Wikipedia Commons: Tobi87: page 15 (bottom);
    Library of Congress: page 17
All other images by Shutterstock.com

Illustrations:
Barabara Bedell: page 14 (top)
Samara Parent: pages 4–5, 6, 8, 20
Bonna Rouse: pages 14 (bottom), 16
Margaret Salter: page 15 (top)

Cover description: Beautiful rock formations like the stone arch can be found in the desert in Utah. Totem poles like this one in Alaska are examples of native art and beliefs. San Francisco, California, is a busy port city on the San Fransisco Bay. Recently cut pine logs wait to be transported.

Title page description: The Golden Gate Bridge is a suspension bridge located in San Francisco, California. It stretches across the San Francisco Bay where it meets the Pacific Ocean.

Library and Archives Canada Cataloguing in Publication

Walker, Robert, 1980-
    What's in the West? / Robert Walker.

(All around the U.S.)
Includes index.
Issued also in electronic formats.
ISBN 978-0-7787-1827-7 (bound).--ISBN 978-0-7787-1833-8 (pbk.)

    1. West (U.S.)--Juvenile literature. I. Title. II. Series: All around the U.S.

F591.W34 2012   j978   C2011-904849-3

Library of Congress Cataloging-in-Publication Data

Walker, Robert, 1980-
 What's in the West? / Robert Walker.
    p. cm. -- (All around the U.S.)
 Includes index.
 ISBN 978-0-7787-1827-7 (reinforced library binding : alk. paper) -- ISBN 978-0-7787-1833-8 (pbk. : alk. paper) -- ISBN 978-1-4271-8781-9 (electronic pdf) -- ISBN 978-1-4271-9598-2 (electronic html)
 1. West (U.S.)--Juvenile literature. I. Title. II. Series.

F591.W2573 2012
978--dc23
                                           2011026693

Crabtree Publishing Company

Printed in Canada/082011/MA20110714

Published in Canada
Crabtree Publishing
616 Welland Ave.
St. Catharines, ON
L2M 5V6

Published in the United States
Crabtree Publishing
PMB 59051
350 Fifth Avenue, 59th Floor
New York, New York 10118

Published in the United Kingdom
Crabtree Publishing
Maritime House
Basin Road North, Hove
BN41 1WR

Published in Australia
Crabtree Publishing
3 Charles Street
Coburg North
VIC 3058

CONTENTS

Words that are defined in the glossary are in **bold** type
the first time they appear in the text.

The United States of America

The United States of America is the third-largest country in the world. It covers most of the southern part of North America. It is surrounded by Canada to the north, the Atlantic Ocean in the east, Mexico in the south, and the Pacific Ocean in the west. There are 50 states in the United States, as well as the District of Columbia, which is the nation's capital.

REGIONS OF THE UNITED STATES

The United States is divided into regions. There are five regions in the United States: the northeast, southeast, midwest, southwest, and the west. A region is an area that has one or more common characteristics or features.

Time and Place

Time zones are regions that share the same time on a clock. Zip codes are numbers that indicate different mail regions for the postal service.

WHY DO WE HAVE REGIONS?

The world is a big place, and breaking it up into smaller pieces makes it easier to understand. There are many different kinds of regions. Geographic regions share landforms such as mountains and rivers. Political regions show us the different countries, states, and cities. There are also industrial and agricultural regions, which show where things are made and grown.

The Western Region

There are 11 states in the western region. These are broken down into sub-regions called the Mountain and Pacific States. The Mountain States are Colorado, Idaho, Montana, Nevada, Utah, and Wyoming. They are further inland. The Pacific States are Washington, Oregon, California, Alaska, and Hawaii. They border the Pacific Ocean.

GREAT HEIGHTS

The Mountain States get their name from the great number of mountains that cover their landscapes. Except for Nevada, all of the Mountain States are part of the Rocky Mountain range. The Rocky Mountain range is the biggest system of mountains in North America. It runs from the United States/Mexico border into northern Canada. There are peaks along the range that reach over 14,000 feet (4300 meters).

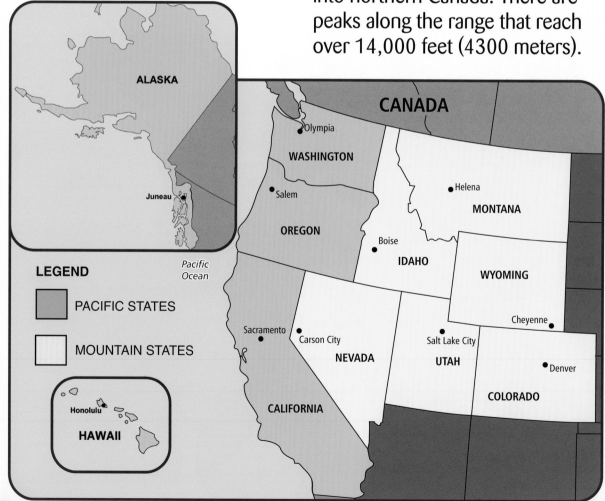

ALASKA

Juneau

LEGEND

Pacific Ocean

PACIFIC STATES

MOUNTAIN STATES

Honolulu

HAWAII

CANADA

Olympia

WASHINGTON

Salem

OREGON

Helena

MONTANA

Boise

IDAHO

WYOMING

Cheyenne

Sacramento

Carson City

Salt Lake City

NEVADA

UTAH

Denver

CALIFORNIA

COLORADO

A VIEW OF THE OCEAN

Most of the Pacific States run south from the Canadian border, all the way to Mexico. They have very diverse **climates**. The northern-most state, Alaska, is dominated by a subarctic landscape, covered in snow and rain most of the year. Meanwhile, the island state of Hawaii is a tropical paradise, with sunshine and warm weather almost year round.

High and Low

The Mountain States are not all peaks and valleys. The eastern sections of states such as Montana and Wyoming are a part of the Great Plains.

The sunny shores of Hawaii (left) and the snowy stretches of Alaska (below) are separated from the rest of the U.S. by ocean and land.

The Lay of the Land

All of the states in the western region have a wide variety of landforms, or natural features. The Sierra Nevada mountain range runs through both the Pacific California and Mountain Nevada states. In Washington, rain forests cover the mountains of the west, and descend into the dry grasslands of the east.

THE HIGHEST PEAKS

The western region is home to some of the biggest and longest mountain ranges in North America. The Rocky Mountains run from Alaska all the way to Wyoming and beyond. Many peaks reach 13,000 feet (3,962 m) in height. Mount Elbert in Colorado is over 14,000 feet (4,267 m) high. The tallest mountain in North America is Mount McKinley in Alaska. This frosty giant is over 20,000 feet (6,100 m) high. It is so cold and so tall that it spends most of its time covered in clouds!

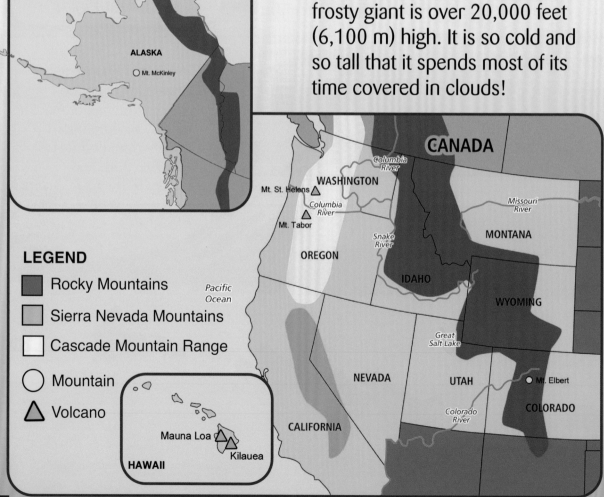

ALASKA
O Mt. McKinley

CANADA

Columbia River

WASHINGTON
Mt. St. Helens △
Columbia River
△ Mt. Tabor

Missouri River

Snake River

MONTANA

OREGON

IDAHO

WYOMING

Pacific Ocean

Great Salt Lake

LEGEND
- ■ Rocky Mountains
- ■ Sierra Nevada Mountains
- ■ Cascade Mountain Range
- ○ Mountain
- △ Volcano

NEVADA

UTAH

O Mt. Elbert

Colorado River

COLORADO

Mauna Loa △
△
Kilauea

CALIFORNIA

HAWAII

8

SLEEPING GIANTS

The Mountains of the western region may be pretty to look at, but some have a violent history—they were once fiery volcanoes! Volcanoes are openings where super hot molten rock from deep underground rise to Earth's surface. Most volcanoes in the western region are dormant, or no longer active. They are quiet now and even safe to live near. Mount Tabor in Oregon even has a city park built on it. There are some volcanoes in the western region that are still active. Hawaii has several active volcanoes, such as Kilauea and Mauna Loa. Washington has an active volcano of its own. In 1980, Mount St. Helens erupted, and over fifty people were killed. Scientists work very hard to keep a close eye on these potential dangers.

The still-active Mount St. Helens in Washington attracts many visitors every year.

Cracks Underground

Earth's surface is built upon huge plates of rock which are always moving. A break in these gigantic plates is called a fault. One of the biggest faults is the San Andreas, which crosses underneath California. When broken plates collide, they cause earthquakes on the surface.

The Lowest Valleys

Between the tall peaks of the western mountain ranges lay stretches of deserts, grasslands, and plains. Deserts are very hot and dry regions covered in sand. Mountain states such as Nevada and Utah are famous for their desert landscapes, which feature interesting rock formations. The grasslands and plains of the western region lay mostly in the eastern parts of states such as Montana and Wyoming. The land there is so flat you can see for miles in any direction.

THE ISLAND STATE

Hawaii has the distinction of being the only state made up entirely of islands. Hawaii is an **archipelago**, or string of islands, that are grouped together in the Pacific Ocean. The only way to travel between the islands is by boat. "It may be far away from the rest of its western states, but Hawaii shares the same variety of mountainous and low-lying landscapes.

Beautiful rock formations can be seen in Utah's deserts.

WATER, WATER, EVERYWHERE

The vast coastline of the west may be impressive—but it does not stop there! Huge lakes and massive rivers stretch out across the region. They range in size from small quiet streams to incredibly fast moving whitewater areas. Beginning in the Rocky Mountains, the Missouri River is the longest in the United States, reaching close to 2,500 miles (4,020 km) in length.

THE GREAT SALT LAKE

The Great Salt Lake in Utah is the biggest inland saltwater lake in the country. It is almost 75 miles (121 km) long and 35 miles (56 km) wide. The lake is even saltier than ocean water. In fact, it is so salty that no fish can live in it.

Death Valley

California's Death Valley is the lowest area of land in North America. It lays almost 300 feet below **sea level**. It is also one of the hottest and driest places in the entire United States.

Only algae is able to survive in the waters of the Great Salt Lake.

How's the Weather?

Rain, wind, temperature, snow— all of these things make up the climate, or weather, of a region. The climate in the western region can be very different and people, plants, and animals have found ways to survive in them all.

IN THE SOIL

In states such as Washington and Oregon, rainy mountainous regions are perfect for rainforest trees to grow in. The low-lying areas of the western region tend to be drier and warmer. These arid climates are home to tropical fruits such as pineapples in Hawaii, and prairie wheats and grains in Wyoming and Idaho. Even the frosty subarctic and desert areas have vegetation that grows there. Not all of Alaska is covered in snow. Spruce trees and even Forget-Me-Nots, the state flower, are able to grow there.

California has a very diverse climate. The Joshua trees (left) of the Mojave Desert need little water to grow. However, the giant redwoods (above) grow hundreds of feet high in the rainy Sequoia National Park.

LIVING HERE

Humans are very flexible when it comes to adjusting to a climate. A T-shirt and shorts are ideal for sunny southern California. Farmers prefer flannel and wide-brimmed hats on the plains in eastern Wyoming and Colorado. And if you live in the rainy coastal area of Washington, you better have an umbrella. Most people prefer to live in the more temperate climates of the region, but there are some who are willing to brave the extreme hot and cold areas as well. Most foods cannot be grown in these two extremes, which means it must be brought in from other places. Special clothing is also required to survive the coldest winters and the hottest summers.

Built for the Weather

Animals are naturally made to live in their different climates. Caribou have thick fur coats which helps them survive in very cold climates. They also have wide flat hooves that help them walk in deep snow.

The First People

European explorers did not really "discover" North America, people had already been living here for thousands of years! Native Americans are the **indigenous**, or orignal, people of North America. The western region was home to many different groups of Native Americans, each with their own way of life.

Native peoples used large nets to catch fish and other foods from lakes, rivers, and streams.

ALONG THE COAST

Living near the ocean and the waterways that ran inland meant a life of fishing. Most coastal nations, or groups, of Native Americans were excellent fishermen. They not only caught smaller fish such as salmon, they even went after whales! Some nations such as the Chumash (right) relied on hunting and gathering roots, seeds, berries, and acorns for food. They lived in cone-shaped huts that were covered in layers of grass, straw, or reeds.

The Real First Settlers

Native Americans first moved to this continent thousands of years ago. They crossed over from Asia to Alaska on land that is now covered by the Pacific Ocean.

IN MOUNTAIN COUNTRY

Native Americans living in mountainous regions used the rocky terrain to their advantage. The over hanging cliffs provided protection from the weather. Nations such as the Anasazi were known for their stonework, which included making homes. Some nations relied on hunting and gathering for food, while others made the move to simple farming. Shoshoni males became an adult when they were sent out into the wild to have a vision that would show them their "guardian spirit," or protector in life.

ON THE PLAINS

Life on the grasslands and desert regions meant a lot of moving around for most nations. They relied on hunting animals such as buffalo, which meant following the herds across the landscape. Animals were more than just food to some nations such as the Cheyenne. They used every part of the animal. The dried skins were used for shelter and clothing, and even the bones could be used to make tools.

The Anasazi people carved their homes into the cliffs of Mesa Verde, Colorado.

Native peoples dried and stretched the skins of buffalo to make clothes.

Settling in the New World

The western regions were the last to be permanently settled in North America. European conquest of the new world began on the other side of the continent. The development of cities, towns, and industry in the east was well underway by the time settlers began setting their sights west in the mid-1800s. Many saw the West as a wild and untamed wilderness—and they were right. There were many obstacles that awaited those hoping to **colonize** the western region.

GETTING THERE

The first settlers to the West made the journey by land, using a series of trails. Routes such as the Oregon, Mormon, and California trails took settlers into the western region—but each was full of possible dangers. Many got sick or injured, and with no doctors for hundreds of miles, they died. The weather was also working against the settlers on their long trek. It was very dangerous to be caught out in the wilderness when winter set in. It was not until the creation of a cross-country railroad that traveling west became safer.

(left) Many settlers died during the harsh winters on the trip west.
(below) The completion of the cross-country railroad made the trip west safer and faster.

LAST ONE IN

Native Americans had been living in the West for thousands of years. They had no where to go when settlers began pouring into their territory. Some land was purchased from Native American groups, usually in unfair deals. Native Americans were forced from their homes and onto **reservations**. These were usually pieces of land that were no good for farming or hunting. Many Native Americans tried to resist, which led to fierce battles with United States troops.

WHO GETS WHAT?

The United States, Britain, and Spain were also fighting for control of land. During these struggles many of the western region states as we know them today changed hands several times. At one time, the entire western region was under Spanish rule. Slowly, the United States took control of the west, either by buying land or by force. Hawaii was the last state to join the United States. Hawaii became a U.S. territory in 1900, and finally the 50th state in 1959.

Lewis and Clark

Meriwether Lewis and William Clark were two explorers who helped map out the West. Their efforts helped pave the way for settlers moving to the western region.

Custer's Last Stand was a famous battle between U.S. troops and Native Americans. The Native Americans were trying to stop the U.S. troops from taking their land.

Where People Live

People consider many different things when deciding where to live. Most prefer a comfortable climate and landscape. Access to jobs, a home, and services such as water and electricity also play a role. The largest populations of people tend to be in and around cities and towns. Some prefer to live in rural areas, away from the hustle and bustle of city life.

Close enough

A growing trend in population distribution is people working in large cities, while living in smaller cities and towns that surround them. These smaller communities are called suburbs.

BIG CITY LIVING

Life in a metropolitan area, or large city, means jobs, entertainment, professional sports teams, and other things people enjoy. It also allows for access to public transportation such as buses and subways. It can be very crowded, however, as most major cities occupy relatively less space to the number of people living there. Los Angeles, California, has a population of over 3.5 million people living in an area of around 466 square miles (1207 sq. km)— that's almost 8,000 people per square mile (2.6 sq. km)!

The Grove is a huge mall in Los Angeles, California. It has stores, movie theaters, and even its own trolley!

WIDE OPEN SPACES

Smaller cities and towns have more natural features, such as mountains and lakes, that people enjoy. The city of Portland, Oregon, has a population of over half a million people living in an area of around 134 square miles (347 sq. km)—and almost 15 percent of that is parks and open spaces.

EXTREME LIVING

Some people enjoy living in the rugged wilderness. Alaska occupies around 663,267 square miles (1,718,000 sq. km), with less than 700,000 people living there. Barrow, Alaska is the most northern (and one of the coldest) cities in the United States. It is just 350 miles (563 km) from the North Pole. Between November and January there is no sunshine, but over 4,000 people still choose to live there.

CLOSE TO WATER

Most large cities today began as small settlements close to the ocean or a waterway. Years ago people depended on rivers and lakes for travel and trade. Today, many industries still depend on water to move goods from place to place. San Francisco, California is an example of a big city built around a busy port.

San Francisco grew on a peninsula between the Pacific Ocean and San Francisco Bay.

Portland is home to Forest Park, the country's biggest urban forest area.

Making Use of the Environment

Everything we use in our daily life, from tables to cars, comes from **natural resources**. Natural resources include water, trees, and metals in the earth. The western region is rich with a wide variety of natural resources that we rely on.

GOOD FOR GROWING

The rainy western areas of Washington and Oregon are perfect conditions for trees to grow. In fact, Oregon produces much of the lumber for the rest of the country. The prairie lands in Wyoming and Idaho are used to grow vegetables, wheat, and other cereal plants. Idaho is also famous for its potatoes. The warm and sunny climate of California produces grapes and other fruits. Hawaii's tropical climate makes it a major producer of pineapples, sugarcane, and macadamia nuts.

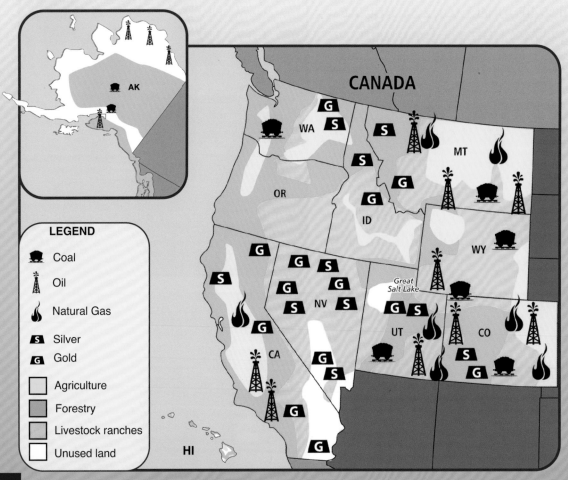

LEGEND

- Coal
- Oil
- Natural Gas
- S Silver
- G Gold
- Agriculture
- Forestry
- Livestock ranches
- Unused land

FISHING AND FARMING

With such a long coastline the western region produces much of the United States' seafood. The ports in Alaska, Washington, and Oregon buzz with boats bringing in loads of salmon and crabs.

The meat we eat and milk we drink has to come from somewhere. Cattle farming, which includes cows, bisons, and yaks, is a large part of the farming industry of western states such as Nevada, Idaho, and Wyoming. Pork, which comes from pigs, is also farmed in the western region.

DIGGING IN THE DIRT

There are many natural resources underground, too. The coal mines in Wyoming produce the most coal in the United States. Gold and silver mines dot the Nevada and Colorado landscapes. Other important **minerals** such as copper, coal, and lead can be found in the western region, along with natural gas and oil. The biggest oilfield in North America was discovered in northern Alaska. Almost 800 miles of pipe carry the oil to a shipping area in Valdez, Alaska, in the south.

(left) Crab boats return to port in Newport, Oregon.
(below) Otters were just one of the many animals that suffered from the Exxon Valdez oil spill.

A Big Spill

In 1989, the oil tanker, Exxon Valdez, spilled over 10 million gallons (37,850 kiloliters) of oil into Alaskan waters. It caused an oil slick that killed hundreds of thousands of animals, including fish, birds, and seals.

Jobs and Wealth in the West

Natural resources play a large part in the economies of the western region states—but there's more to the industries of the west than oil and agriculture. Many industries are continuing to grow and develop across the Mountain and Pacific states.

ACROSS THE SEA

A long coastline makes the western region a prime location for ocean **harbors**. These shipping ports send and receive goods between the United States and the rest of the world. Seattle, Washington, is home to the largest **containerports** in the United States.

TECHNOLOGY

Washington and Oregon produce more than just lumber. Washington is also home to the Boeing Company, which makes jets. Boeing is the largest employer in the whole state. The Boeing assembly plant in Everett, Washington, is the largest building in the world. The Oregon electronics industry produces computers, calculators, and other electronic equipment. Most of the electronics industry is centered in Portland.

Shipyards line Seattle's coastline.

THE SERVICE INDUSTRY

Any business that provides a service without actually making something is a part of the service industry. The service industry is the biggest state employer in places such as Utah, California, and Colorado. Jobs in the service industry include government jobs at national parks or in the **military**. It also includes jobs such as doctors, teachers, store clerks, and theme park employees.

ENTERTAINMENT

Nevada is known by many as the "Entertainment Capital of the World." Centered on tourism, cities such as Las Vegas are brimming with casinos, theaters, and theme parks. Millions of people visit every year from all around the world.

THE GOODS WE USE

Montana is a major producer of hydroelectricity. About 40 percent of the state's electricity comes from hydroelectric power. Wyoming makes use of its sugar beets by refining, or changing, them into sugar. And Boise, Idaho, is home to one of the United States' biggest producers of wood products.

Workers at Disneyland, in California, help to provide fun and entertainment for vacationing families.

Most of the attractions in Las Vegas are open 24 hours a day, seven days a week.

Plenty to Do

The beautiful variety of landscapes across the western region make it a popular place for tourists. There are also many human-made attractions to draw people in from across the country and around the world.

THE GREAT OUTDOORS

State and national parks are appealing to sightseers and hikers who enjoy the mountain peaks, rolling hills, and valleys. The slopes of Colorado, Idaho, and Utah draw millions of skiers every year. Alaska even offers tourism for the hardiest travelers. Tours of its 15 national parks and 16 wildlife refuges as well as **glaciers** and ice fields are very popular.

A TROPICAL GETAWAY

Hawaii's economy is based mostly on tourism. Millions of people travel there every year to enjoy its beaches and exotic natural features. Visitors can go scuba diving or surfing, hike the hills and dormant volcanoes, or just stretch out on the beach. Locals also put on elaborate displays of native dance, music, and art.

(top) Locals perform a traditional Hawaiian dance for tourists.

(left) The snowy peaks of Colorado's mountains are ideal for skiing and snowboarding.

HISTORIC SITES

Monuments celebrating U.S. history are very popular for tourists looking to experience some of the nation's rich past. Utah is home to the Golden Spike National Monument, which marks the completion of the first **transcontinental** railroad. The Hoover Dam is one of the largest in the world. It is over 1,244 feet (379 m) long and 726 feet (221 m) tall and took over five years to build.

EXTREME SPORTS

For the more adventurous tourist, the western region offers the chance to enjoy potentially dangerous sports such as rock climbing and whitewater rafting. The Owens River Gorge in California and Red Rock Canyon in Nevada are very popular climbing destinations. Utah and Idaho's rushing mountain rivers attract rafting enthusiasts.

THE CITY THAT NEVER SLEEPS

Tens of millions of people travel to Las Vegas, Nevada, every year. Most of the attractions are open 24 hours a day. Tourists can gamble at casinos, take in a music or magic show, or enjoy one of the circuses or amusement parks.

Old Faithful

Yellowstone National Park features Old Faithful (right). It is a hot spring **geyser** that erupts every 33 to 90 minutes, shooting steam and hot water high into the air.

Western Culture

The culture of a people can be the way they live, what they do, and what they believe in. Like most other regions in the United States, the western region is a **mosaic** of the different cultures of people from across the country and around the world.

THE ARTS

Western art dates back all the way to the first Native Americans. One of most popular forms of Native art is the totem pole. Carved from a tree, totem poles are tall and colorful. They feature the animals and other parts of a nation's **mythology**, or beliefs. Some were used to identify different nations, others were used to carry the remains of dead loved ones. Modern day western art includes everything from paintings and carvings to music and theater. Much of it reflects the wild and natural landscape of the western region. Works of art are mostly kept on display at museums, while live performances of music and plays are held in public theaters.

A native totem pole stands tall in Ketchlkan, Alaska.

DIFFERENT WAYS OF LIFE

The customs of a people depends on their beliefs and history. In many cases, people with similar customs will stay close together. In the mid-1800s thousands of people of the **Mormon** faith moved across the country to the western region. They settled in what is now Utah, primarily around Salt Lake City. The Mormon population in the city continued to grow, and now a Large area of the city's downtown is dedicated to the preservation, history, and celebration of the faith.

CELEBRATIONS

What's the point of having culture if you don't celebrate it? The states of the western region all have special occasions to remember and enjoy important parts of their different cultures. Hawaii's Aloha Festivals are held in autumn. They hold over 300 events on the six major islands. The ten-day event celebrates Hawaii's music, dancing, and history. Idaho holds festivals to celebrate its agriculture, such as the Cherry Festival and Idaho Annual Spud Day.

(top) The colorful floral parade in Honolulu, Hawaii, is part of the Aloha Festivals.

(left) Many buildings in Salt Lake City represent the Mormon faith, such as this Mormon temple.

Welcome to Hollywood

Hollywood is a small **district** in the city of Los Angeles. It began as a Native American Shoshone settlement in the Santa Monica Mountains. Today it is the movie capital of the world. Many people call Hollywood the City of Dreams. Thousands of people flock there every year in the hopes of becoming a part of the movie making business.

BIG SCREENS EVERYWHERE

Hollywood produces the majority of films in the entire world. Movies made in Hollywood are translated into different languages so audiences in other countries can enjoy them.

(top) The Hollywood sign in Los Angeles is a famous landmark located in the Santa Monica Mountains.

(bottom) Sony Pictures Entertainment produces some of the most popular movies in the world.

MOVIE STARS

When a movie becomes popular, so do the actors that are in it. Hollywood actors can become very popular. These actors are called celebrities. Celebrity watching is a large part of North American culture. People follow the lives of celebrities with the same kind of enthusiasm that people in other countries do for kings and queens. People love to read about movie stars in gossip magazines and in the newspapers, and watch them in interviews on television. Many movie stars have fan clubs, where members share their similar interest.

TELLING STORIES

Movies are an exciting and fun way to tell stories to a large audience, whether it be real or make believe. Some movies are based on true stories about North America or people and cultures from around the world. Movies made in Hollywood influence culture not only in North America but many other countries as well.

From "Silent" to "Talkie"

The first movies were in black and white and had no sound. This meant actors had to use their body movements to relay what they were "saying." It took years for filmmakers to figure out how to add sound to movies. The first "talkie" was made in the 1920s.

Celebrities Angelina Jolie and Brad Pitt sign autographs for crowds of adoring fans.

Timeline

1803 - Montana, Wyoming, and Colorado are bought from France by the U.S.

1805 - Lewis and Clark reach the Pacific Ocean

1811 - The first American settlement is founded west of the Rocky Mountains

1837 - Henry Spalding plants the first Idaho potato

1843 - Thousands of settlers cross the Oregon Trail to settle in the west

1846 - Great Britain gives up control of Idaho

1848 - California becomes U.S. territory after the Mexican-American War

1849 - The California gold rush begins

1850 - California becomes the 31st state

1858 - The discovery of silver in Nevada

1859 - Oregon becomes the 33rd state

1861 - The first east-to-west telegraph line is completed

1864 - Nevada becomes the 36th state

1869 - The first transcontinental railroad is completed

1872 - The oldest national park, Yellowstone, is founded

1876 - Native warriors defeat U.S. troops at the Battle of Little Bighorn

1876 - Colorado becomes the 38th state

1889 - Montana becomes the 41st state

1889 - Washington becomes the 42nd state

1890 - Idaho becomes the 43rd state

1890 - Wyoming becomes the 44th state

1893 - Queen Liliuolaka loses power and Hawaii comes under U.S. control

1896 - Utah becomes the 45th state

1906 - The Denver U.S. Mint produces its first coins

1910 - The first movie is shot in Hollywood

1931 - Nevada legalizes gambling

1959 - Alaska becomes the 49th state

1959 - Hawaii becomes the 50th state

1968 - America's biggest oil field is discovered in Alaska

1980 - Mount St. Helens erupts

1989 - Oil tanker, Exxon Valdez, spills in Alaskan waters

1991 - Barbara Roberts is elected the first female governor of Oregon

Find Out More

BOOKS

Our 50 United States, Renee Skelton by Jaime Joyce, HarperCollins, 2006.

The New Big Book of America by Todd Davis and Marc Frey, RunningPress, 2002.

Welcome to the United States of America by Meredith Costain and Paul Collins, Chelsea House Publishers, 2001.

Countries of the World: United States by Elden Croy, National Geographic Society, 2010.

WEBSITES

Find out more about the West and America's other regions at:
www.eduplace.com/ss/socsci/tx/books/bkd/ilessons/

Discover everything you need to know about America's 50 states at:
www.factmonster.com/states.html

Learn about individual state flowers, flags, famous people, and more at this interesting site:
http://www.50states.com/

Glossary

archipelago A large group of islands

climate The long-term weather conditions in an area, including temperature, rainfall, and wind

colonize Moving to a new place and taking control of it

containerport A port specially equipped to handle cargo in containers

district An area of a city, such as a group of neighborhoods

geyser A body of hot water underground that boils over and shoots up into the air

glacier A large, slow-moving body of ice

harbor A part of a coast where boats are safe from wind and big ocean waves

indigenous People that are originally from a region or area

military The soldiers that protect a country

mineral A non-living substance found in nature that helps plants and animals grow

Mormon A follower of the religion the Church of Jesus Christ of Latter-Day Saints

mosaic A mix of people of different races and beliefs

mythology A set of stories that is made up to explain unusual events

natural resource Things from nature, such as trees, water, and minerals

reservation An area of land Native Americans were forced to live on by the United States government

sea level The height of the sea compared to things on land

transcontinental Something that crosses an entire continent

Index